SPIES

[CIVIL WAR] SPIES

by TIM O'SHEI

Consultant:
Jan Goldman, EdD
Founding Board Member
International Intelligence Ethics Association
Washington, D.C.

Capstone
press

Mankato, Minnesota

Edge Books are published by Capstone Press,
151 Good Counsel Drive, P.O. Box 669, Mankato, Minnesota 56002.
www.capstonepress.com

Library of Congress Cataloging-in-Publication Data
O'Shei, Tim.
    Civil War spies / by Tim O'Shei.
    p. cm. — (Edge books. Spies)
    Summary: "Discusses the history of spying during the Civil War" — Provided
by publisher.
    Includes bibliographical references and index.
    ISBN-13: 978-1-4296-1306-4 (hardcover)
    ISBN-10: 1-4296-1306-8 (hardcover)
    1. United States — History — Civil War, 1861–1865 — Secret service —
Juvenile literature. 2. United States — History — Civil War, 1861–1865 —
Underground movements — Juvenile literature. 3. Spies — United States —
History — 19th century — Juvenile literature. 4. Spies — Confederate States
of America — History — Juvenile literature. 5. Spies — United States —
Biography — Juvenile literature. 6. Spies — Confederate States of America —
Biography — Juvenile literature. I. Title.
E608.O84 2008
973.7'86 — dc22   2007033576

Editorial Credits
Angie Kaelberer, editor; Bob Lentz, book designer; Jo Miller, photo researcher

Photo Credits
AP Images/Alexander Gardner, 7; Old Courthouse Museum, File, 26
Capstone Press Archives, 14
Corbis, 13; Alexander Gardner, 8; Bettmann, cover, 21, 25
Historical Photograph Collection, Digital Library and Archives,
    University Libraries, Virginia Polytechnic Institute and State University, 17
Library of Congress, 11, 19, 22
Shutterstock/Aga, 1, 10; Feng Yu, 9
Special Collections Research Center, Swem Library, College of William
    and Mary, 4
SuperStock Inc., 28

1 2 3 4 5 6 13 12 11 10 09 08

[TABLE OF CONTENTS]

———◆———

CRAZY BET, THE SPY

> Elizabeth Van Lew was 42 years old when the Civil War began.

Crazy. There was no other way to say it. Elizabeth "Bet" Van Lew was simply crazy. She walked the streets of Richmond, Virginia, singing out loud. Sometimes she carried on a full conversation, though there was no one next to her. Her curly hair shot wildly in all directions. Her blue eyes fluttered about. She looked crazy, she acted crazy, and that's what people called her: "Crazy Bet."

PRISON VISITS

Van Lew's behavior wasn't the only reason people thought she was strange. She also liked visiting prisoners of war. At the time, the United States was involved in the Civil War (1861–1865). The North, called the Union, fought the South, or the Confederacy.

Richmond was the capital of the Confederacy. Captured Union soldiers were held in Libby Prison in Richmond. Van Lew regularly brought baskets of food and medicine to the Union prisoners.

Though Confederate officials were suspicious of Van Lew's prison visits, they weren't worried. Van Lew was crazy, they figured. How could she cause any harm?

NOT SO CRAZY

Confederate officials didn't know the whole story. Van Lew's visits weren't social calls. She talked to prisoners about what they had seen on the battlefield. She gathered details about the Confederate troops and passed them to the Union. She also hid Union prisoners who escaped from the prison. Union General Ulysses S. Grant praised Van Lew's efforts. He said her information was the most valuable he received from Richmond during the war.

Van Lew's strangeness was only an act. She wasn't crazy. She was a spy.

> About 50,000 Union prisoners served sentences at Libby Prison in Richmond from 1861 to 1864.

CHAPTER 2

DIVIDED BY SLAVERY

LEARN ABOUT:
> Slavery leads to war
> Racist beliefs
> Women as spies

> Abraham Lincoln was elected president of the United States in 1860.

In the mid-1800s, the United States was divided into slave states and free states. Most slave states were in the South. Slaves could try to escape to the North. But if they were caught, they could be returned to their owners.

Some slaves succeeded in escaping to the North. Several laws were passed in an effort to come to an agreement on slavery. None worked. Also, Southerners wanted to make their own laws.

Southerners' unhappiness grew stronger in 1860, when Abraham Lincoln was elected president. Lincoln was against slavery. He also was determined to keep the country together. In February 1861, several southern states declared themselves free of the United States. They decided to secede, forming the Confederate States of America. They elected Jefferson Davis as their president.

Two months later, Confederate soldiers fired on Fort Sumter in South Carolina. With that attack, the Civil War began.

secede

to formally withdraw from a group or an organization

CHALLENGES OF WAR

The North had many advantages in the Civil War. It had factories to make weapons and railroads to transport supplies. Most of the country's food came from the North.

Spying, though, was easier for the South. The Confederacy had plenty of chances to slip spies inside the large Union government. Plus, most of the battles took place in the South. Union spies in the South faced constant danger.

SPY FACT

The first southern states to secede were South Carolina, Mississippi, Florida, Alabama, Georgia, Louisiana, and Texas.

SPY FILES: A BALLOON VIEW

Today, military officials often use spy planes or satellites to collect information. During the Civil War, the Union used hot air balloons for the same purpose. The balloons floated as high as 5,000 feet (1,500 meters) in the air. They were attached to the ground by a very long cable. A spy in the balloon's basket studied distant troop movements and geography. A telegraph wire snaked from the balloon to the ground. The wire allowed observers to transmit information quickly.

UNLIKELY SPIES

Civil War spies were often people no one would suspect. The Union sometimes used African Americans as spies. Back then, racism was widespread. Many people didn't believe African Americans were smart or creative. Those incorrect beliefs worked in favor of the Union. Slaves and servants could listen in on conversations without raising suspicions.

Both sides used women as spies. At that time, women were rarely considered a threat. They had no voting rights. Few held jobs. Many people believed women's most important duty was serving their husbands and families. That idea helped some women become excellent spies. Women could move about and talk to soldiers openly. Few people ever suspected they were spying.

racism

the belief that one race is better than another race

> Taking care of sick or wounded soldiers gave
women chances to gather information.

CHAPTER 3

MISSIONS OF TRICKERY

LEARN ABOUT:
> Servant spies
> Changed identities
> An assassination stopped

> Mary Bowser attended school in Philadelphia before becoming a Union spy.

Good spies are great observers who blend into their surroundings. Consider Mary Bowser, who was a former slave of the Van Lew family. After the family freed Bowser, Elizabeth Van Lew helped her get a job in Richmond. Bowser became a servant in the home of Confederate President Jefferson Davis.

While Bowser tended to her duties, Davis and his assistants spoke freely about their war plans. They likely thought Bowser couldn't read, write, or even understand what they were talking about. How wrong they were.

Bowser was very smart. She was said to have a powerful memory. She remembered tiny details about photos and documents. She soaked up this **intelligence** and shared it with Union leaders.

Bowser wasn't the only spy close to Davis. Davis' carriage driver, William Jackson, also gathered intelligence for the Union government.

intelligence

sensitive information collected or analyzed by spies

A SPY IN DISGUISE

The Confederates also slipped spies into powerful places. Thomas Conrad was known in Washington as a Confederate supporter. Conrad changed his hair, beard, and clothing so that nobody recognized him.

Conrad became friends with people in the War Department. He browsed through the building at lunchtime, when many people were gone. He helped himself to information left on desks. Conrad then delivered Union battle plans to the Confederates. His information helped the Confederates win the Battle of Fredericksburg in December 1862.

SPY FACT

In 1995, Mary Bowser was elected to the U.S. Army Intelligence Hall of Fame.

> Thomas Conrad changed the style of his hair and beard when he became a spy.

THE DENTAL SPY

In 1862, Benjamin Stringfellow moved to Alexandria, Virginia, to set up a spy ring for the Confederacy. Alexandria was only a few miles from Washington, D.C. Stringfellow and his agents spied on the Union government in Washington.

Stringfellow took a new name, Edward Delcher. He got a job working as a dental assistant. Agents from his ring came to the office to get dental work done. They left behind valuable intelligence. Sometimes this information was as simple as newspaper stories filled with details about Union battle plans.

Stringfellow gathered the intelligence into a report that he left outside the dentist's office. Each night, a messenger picked up the report. But one day, Stringfellow learned that the dentist was going to turn him in. Stringfellow fled Alexandria, but he continued spying for the South until the end of the war.

SPY FILES: MESSAGES IN CODE

Thousands of miles of telegraph lines covered both the North and the South. Spies, however, rarely used the wires. Instead, they used secret messengers or creative codes.

An escaped slave named Dabney worked on the Union side of the North-South border. He took messages from his wife, who worked on the Confederate side of the line. She signaled troop movements to him by hanging laundry in a certain order.

> Confederate spies blended in well in the large city of Washington, D.C.

A CHARMING BELLE

Seventeen-year-old Belle Boyd was both pretty and clever. Even though she supported the Confederacy, Boyd attended dances and parties hosted by Union soldiers. She used her charm to trick the Union soldiers into sharing secrets. Boyd learned about battle plans, troop numbers, and troop locations.

In May 1862, Boyd learned Confederate troops were near Front Royal, Virginia. The Union Army controlled this town. From her Union contacts, Boyd knew only a small number of Union soldiers protected the town. As the fighting broke out, Boyd ran through the gunfire to give her news to a Confederate officer.

Armed with Boyd's information, the Confederates marched into Front Royal. During the battle and others that followed, they took 3,000 Union prisoners. They also gained weapons and supplies worth thousands of dollars.

> Union soldiers didn't suspect beautiful Belle Boyd of spying.

A SPY NAMED ROSE

Confederate supporter Rose O'Neal Greenhow was a wealthy widow living in Washington, D.C. Greenhow built a spy ring that included Union soldiers, other women, a banker, and a dentist.

> In 1862, Greenhow and her daughter were held in Old Capitol Prison in Washington, D.C.

In July 1861, Greenhow learned the Union planned an attack in Manassas, Virginia. She sent word to Confederate leaders, who sent extra soldiers to Manassas. The battle that followed is known as the First Battle of Bull Run. It was an important Confederate victory.

Detectives from the Pinkerton Detective Agency arrested Greenhow in August 1861. They planned to have Greenhow continue running her spy ring. That way, Union officials could catch other Confederate spies. But Greenhow's 8-year-old daughter, Rose, ruined the plan. Young Rose ran from her house screaming, "Mother's been arrested!"

Even in prison, Greenhow managed to communicate with her Confederate contacts. Finally, Union officials sent her to Richmond. Jefferson Davis then sent her to Europe to ask for support for the Confederacy. In 1864, Greenhow was returning to the United States by ship. She drowned when the ship sank off the North Carolina coast.

PINKERTON'S BEST MAN

Detective Allan Pinkerton ran a spy ring for the Union. Timothy Webster was one of Pinkerton's best agents. Webster moved from Illinois to Maryland. There, he posed as a Confederate supporter.

In 1861, Webster learned about a plan to **assassinate** Abraham Lincoln. The new president was traveling to Washington, D.C., to take office. Confederate supporters planned to kill Lincoln as he switched trains in Baltimore, Maryland. Based on that tip, Pinkerton was able to stop the assassination attempt.

Webster kept sending valuable information north. But that ended in 1862, when two captured Union spies gave away Webster's identity. The Confederates were shocked and angry. They killed Webster by hanging him.

assassinate

to murder a person who is well known or important, such as a president

> Allan Pinkerton served as a police officer before becoming a detective and a Union spy.

CHAPTER 4

THE FINAL DAYS

LEARN ABOUT:
> Last battles
> Confederate surrender
> A different kind of spying

> During the siege of Vicksburg, some townspeople hid in caves near the city.

Though Confederate spies scored some successes, the South's military couldn't match the Union Army's strength. The war began turning in the North's favor in May 1863. After a long battle, the Union took control of Vicksburg, Mississippi. The army held the town for six weeks. Taking Vicksburg split the South into two parts and weakened the Confederacy.

The Union's position became even stronger in July 1863. Union troops defeated Confederate forces in the Battle of Gettysburg in Pennsylvania. The loss ended Confederate attempts to invade the North.

SPY FACT

About 620,000 American soldiers died in the Civil War. Another 350,000 civilians also died. Based on the population at that time, it was the deadliest war in U.S. history.

By April 1865, Union troops took control of Richmond. On April 9, the commanders of both armies met in the town of Appomattox Court House, Virginia. Confederate General Robert E. Lee and Union General Ulysses S. Grant signed an agreement of surrender. The Civil War was over.

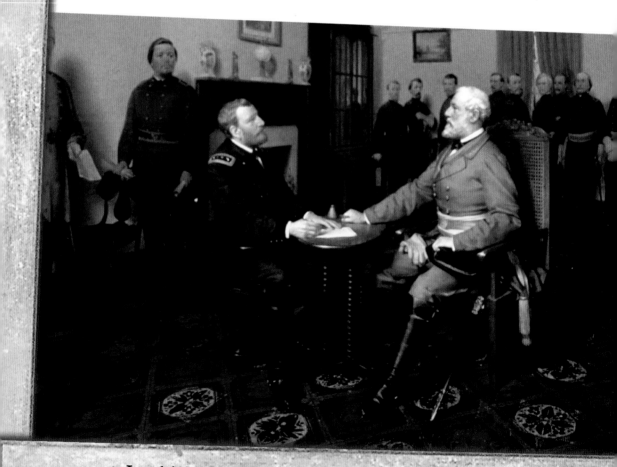

> Lee (right) surrendered to Grant (left) in the parlor of the McLean house in Appomattox Court House.

THE IMPACT OF SPIES

Civil War spying was different from spying in any other U.S. war. Both sides spoke the same language and shared a similar culture. The border separating the North and South was easy to cross. Battle plans were fairly easy to get, whether by reading a newspaper or rummaging through an unguarded office.

Today, military and government information is carefully guarded. The government keeps detailed records on both enemy and friendly countries. Spies who travel into enemy areas do so only with great care.

When the Civil War ended, many spy records were destroyed. The tales that have survived focus largely on women and African Americans. These people bravely used their skills to help the troops they supported. But many more stories of Civil War spying are forever buried in history.

surrender

to give up or admit defeat in battle

GLOSSARY

assassinate (uh-SASS-uh-nate) — to murder a person who is well known or important, such as a president

capital (KAP-uh-tuhl) — a city where a country's government is based

detective (di-TEK-tiv) — a person who investigates crimes or collects information for people

intelligence (in-TEH-luh-juhnss) — sensitive information collected or analyzed by spies

racism (RAY-siz-uhm) — the belief that one race is better than another race

secede (si-SEED) — to formally withdraw from a group or an organization; the Confederate states seceded from the United States at the time of the Civil War.

siege (SEEJ)—the surrounding of a city by troops to cut off movement in or out

surrender (suh-REN-dur) — to give up or admit defeat in battle

READ MORE

Allen, Thomas B. *Harriet Tubman, Secret Agent: How Daring Slaves and Free Blacks Spied for the Union During the Civil War.* Washington, D.C.: National Geographic Society, 2006.

Buranelli, Vincent. *American Spies and Traitors.* Collective Biographies. Berkeley Heights, N.J.: Enslow, 2004.

Coleman, Janet Wyman. *Secrets, Lies, Gizmos, and Spies: A History of Spies and Espionage.* New York: Harry N. Abrams, 2006.

Raatma, Lucia. *Great Women of the Civil War.* We the People. Minneapolis: Compass Point Books, 2005.

INTERNET SITES

FactHound offers a safe, fun way to find Internet sites related to this book. All of the sites on FactHound have been researched by our staff.

Here's how:
1. Visit *www.facthound.com*
2. Choose your grade level.
3. Type in this book ID 1429613068 for age-appropriate sites. You may also browse subjects by clicking on letters, or by clicking on pictures and words.
4. Click on the Fetch It button.

FactHound will fetch the best sites for you!

INDEX